THE HISTORY OF PET LIZARDS

by Alicia Z. Klepeis

pogo

Ideas for Parents and Teachers

Pogo Books let children practice reading informational text while introducing them to nonfiction features such as headings, labels, sidebars, maps, and diagrams, as well as a table of contents, glossary, and index.

Carefully leveled text with a strong photo match offers early fluent readers the support they need to succeed.

Before Reading

- "Walk" through the book and point out the various nonfiction features. Ask the student what purpose each feature serves.
- Look at the glossary together. Read and discuss the words.

Read the Book

- Have the child read the book independently.
- Invite him or her to list questions that arise from reading.

After Reading

- Discuss the child's questions. Talk about how he or she might find answers to those questions.
- Prompt the child to think more. Ask: Do you have a pet lizard or know someone who does? Do you think lizards make good pets? Why or why not?

Pogo Books are published by Jump!
5357 Penn Avenue South
Minneapolis, MN 55419
www.jumplibrary.com

Library of Congress Cataloging-in-Publication Data

Names: Klepeis, Alicia, 1971- author.
Title: The history of pet lizards / by Alicia Z. Klepeis.
Description: Minneapolis, MN: Jump, Inc., [2024]
Series: History of pets | Includes index.
Audience: Ages 7-10
Identifiers: LCCN 2023010409 (print)
LCCN 2023010410 (ebook)
ISBN 9798885246163 (hardcover)
ISBN 9798885246170 (paperback)
ISBN 9798885246187 (ebook)
Subjects: LCSH: Lizards as pets—Juvenile literature.
Lizards as pets—History—Juvenile literature.
Classification: LCC SF459.L5 K54 2024 (print)
LCC SF459.L5 (ebook)
DDC 639.3/95—dc23/eng/20230301
LC record available at https://lccn.loc.gov/2023010409
LC ebook record available at https://lccn.loc.gov/2023010410

Editor: Eliza Leahy
Designer: Molly Ballanger

Photo Credits: fivespots/Shutterstock, cover, 22mr; Kaan Sezer/iStock, 1; Leonardo Garofalo/Shutterstock, 3; irin717/iStock, 4; Elena Sherengovskaya/Shutterstock, 5; Natural Visions/Alamy, 6; showcake/Shutterstock, 7; drknuth/iStock, 8-9; BLUR LIFE 1975/Shutterstock, 10-11; IrinaK/Shutterstock, 12; Gina Kelly/Alamy, 13; Flash-ka/Shutterstock, 14-15tl; Pakjira Rungrojamornkul/Shutterstock, 14-15tr; Opayaza12/Shutterstock, 14-15bl; CSMaster/Shutterstock, 14-15br; Mufti Adi Utomo/Shutterstock, 16-17; mtreasure/iStock, 18-19; ApuuliWorld/iStock, 20-21; Kurit afshen/Shutterstock, 22tl; Robert Eastman/Shutterstock, 22tr; Eric Isselee/Shutterstock, 22ml, 22bl, 22br; GoodFocused/Shutterstock, 23.

Printed in the United States of America at Corporate Graphics in North Mankato, Minnesota.

TABLE OF CONTENTS

CHAPTER 1

LOVE FOR LIZARDS

Have you ever seen a lizard in the wild? Maybe you saw one clinging to a plant. Or perhaps one stopped to warm itself in the Sun.

Lizards are **reptiles**. Most are wild. But some live as pets. How did they become pets? Let's learn!

CHAPTER 2

FROM BUG CATCHER TO PET

Scientists have found lizard **fossils**. Lizards have been around for hundreds of millions of years! How did they start living alongside people?

lizard fossil

In **tropical** areas, wild geckos go into peoples' homes. Why? They follow and hunt insects. This has likely happened for as long as people have had homes. Some people let them stay. They liked that the lizards ate the insects.

green
anole

Not much is known about the earliest pet lizards. People likely caught and kept **native** lizards. One example is the green anole. People collected millions from Louisiana and Florida in the mid-1900s. They sold them to people around the country. The lizards have been popular pets ever since.

Exotic pet lizards have become more popular in recent decades. Bearded dragons are one kind. They are native to Australia. They were kept as pets there. People **smuggled** them out of the country in the 1970s or 1980s. Since then, people have **bred** them in other places.

WHAT DO YOU THINK?

Bearded dragons and blue-tongued lizards are native to Australia. They are the most popular pet lizards there today. Keeping exotic lizards as pets is against the law in Australia. Do you think it should be against the law everywhere? Why or why not?

bearded
dragon

CHAPTER 3

CARING FOR LIZARDS

More than 9 million Americans have pet lizards. Pet lizards often cost less to own than cats or dogs. They are fun to watch. They come in many patterns and colors.

Argentine black and white tegus are popular. A tegu can go for a walk on a leash!

blue-tongued skink

iguana

leopard gecko

chameleon

Skinks are another popular pet. Most can **shed** their tails. Then, they regrow them! Iguanas love to eat vegetables. Leopard geckos shake their tails when they are excited. Chameleons are fun to watch change color.

DID YOU KNOW?

Geckos live on every **continent** except Antarctica. Most lizards don't make noise, but geckos do. They click, chirp, and squeak.

Some experts say people and pet lizards can **bond**. Lizards can be **affectionate**. Some even cuddle on their owners' laps!

Lizards often recognize their owners. Some people train them to come when called. They might use treats, like blueberries or apples, to help.

Pet lizards can live for more than 15 years. It takes work to care for them. They often need heated **terrariums**. Why? Lizards are **cold-blooded**.

Owners need to feed their pet lizards the right foods. Some eat insects. Others eat vegetables and fruits.

TAKE A LOOK!

In which states are lizards the most common pet after cats and dogs? Take a look!

■ **Hawaii**
■ **Nevada**
■ **Texas**
■ **West Virginia**

In the past, some lizards wandered into homes to eat insects. Now people keep many kinds as pets. Would you like a pet lizard?

QUICK FACTS & TOOLS

MOST POPULAR U.S. PET LIZARD BREEDS

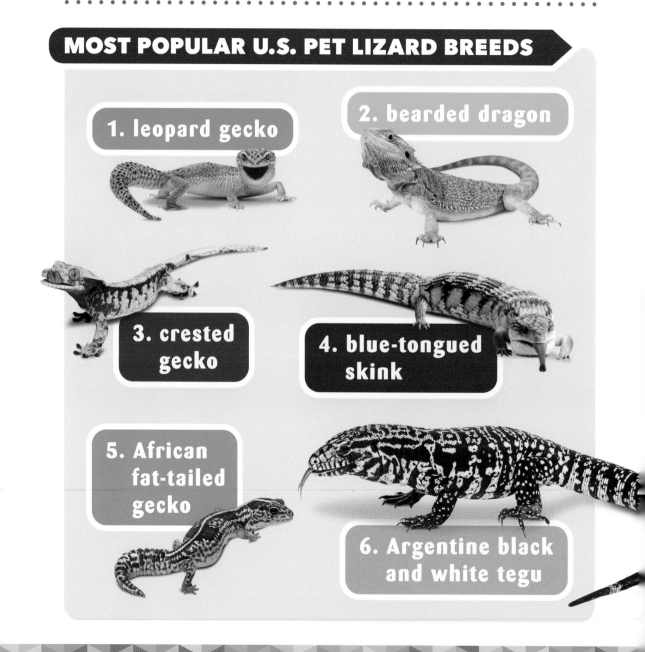

1. leopard gecko

2. bearded dragon

3. crested gecko

4. blue-tongued skink

5. African fat-tailed gecko

6. Argentine black and white tegu

GLOSSARY

affectionate: Loving and friendly.

bond: To form a close relationship with someone, such as a pet or family member.

bred: Kept under controlled conditions to produce more and better quality offspring.

cold-blooded: Having a body temperature that changes according to the temperature of the surroundings.

continent: One of the seven large landmasses on Earth.

exotic: From a faraway country.

fossils: Bones, shells, or traces of animals or plants from millions of years ago.

native: An animal or plant that lives or grows naturally in a certain place.

reptiles: Cold-blooded animals that crawl across the ground or creep on short legs and usually reproduce by laying eggs.

shed: To lose, get rid of, or let something fall.

smuggled: Moved goods into or out of a country illegally.

terrariums: Glass or plastic containers for growing small plants or raising small land animals, such as lizards, in somewhat natural conditions.

tropical: Of or having to do with the hot, rainy area of the earth near the equator.

INDEX

TO LEARN MORE

Finding more information is as easy as 1, 2, 3.

❶ Go to www.factsurfer.com

❷ Enter "thehistoryofpetlizards" into the search box.

❸ Choose your book to see a list of websites.

FACT SURFER